DIRECTORY OF WHOLESALERS

APPAREL

- **Men's Active wear and Sportswear**
  Jon Lauren Apparel Co.
  732-780-2224
  732-780-8823 Fax
  www.jonlauren.com

- **Bras & Panties**
  Tatiana
  941-488-0995
  www.tatianafashions.com

- **Ladies & Men Apparel, Inner & Outerwear**
  Ashley Reed Trading
  212-239-7272
  Email: info@ashleyreed.com

- **Luxury Designer Merchandise**
  Authentic Wholesale
  Handbags, Jewelry, Apparel
  718-252-3849
  www.authenticwholesae.com

- **Seven Seas, Inc.**
  Men and Women's Clothing
  888-373-7726
  www.sevenwholesale.com

- **Wholesale Lingerie**
  JW Intimates
  954-589-2737
  www.jwintimates.com

- **Wholesale Central**
  Women and Men Apparel
  www.wholesalecentral.com

- **Price Grabber**
  Clothing
  www.pricegrabber.com

- **High Fashion Wholesales, Inc.**
  Women, Maternity, Plus, Lingerie
  866-856-8000
  www.offpricefashion.com

- **Liquidators**
  Clothing, more than 500 Products
  www.Liquidation.com

- **RG Riley**
  T – Shirts
  877-576-5447
  www.RGriley.com

- **Primetime Clothing**
  Formal wear, Active wear, Dresses, Plus
  www.primetime.com

- **WFS**
  877-811-4911
  www.wholesalefashionsquare.com

- **Customer Returns, Bulk Purchase only**
  800-224-3141
  www.gencomarketplace.com

- **Fashion world**
  Fashion Handbags, Evening Bags, Wallets, Belts
  213-663-1159
  www.handbagfashion.com

- **Fashion Angeles Wholesale Clothing and Accessories**
  213-746-0035
  www.fashionangeles.com

- **Colin Fashion**
  Wholesale Jewelry and Accessories
  888-563-4411
  www.wholesalejewelry.net

- **Just Simply Unique**
  Popcorn & Mini pleats Ladies Apparel
  813-843-4983
  www.justsimplyunique.com

- **Apparel Candy**
  Contemporary, Women, Misses, Junior, Plus
  877-870-8686
  www.apparelcandy.com

  Art Beat, Inc.
  Specialty designed T - Shirts
  208-743-9351
  www.holycowtees.com

- **Bettencourt Manufacturing**
  Hospital Scrubs and Uniforms
  772-466-4211
  www.trenduniforms.com

- **Sheehan Sales, Inc.,**
  Wholesale Medical Scrubs
  888-707-2782
  www.sheehansales.org
  www.wholesalenursingscrubs.com

- **Main Wholesaler**
  Apparel, etc.
  www.mainwholesaler.com

- **Sharper Uniforms**
  Scrubs & Chef wear up to 7x
  800-356-1757
  www.sharperuniforms.com

- **California Hub**
  Tops, Jeans, Denim Jackets
  888-753-2375
  www.wholesalefashionyetts.com

- **Wholesale Hub**
  Wholesale Clothing Supplies
  877-500-5335
  www.wholesalehub.com

TABLE OF CONTENT

THE ASIAN CONNECTION

- **Dunne Sales, Inc.**
  Sweats, T – Shirts
  828-396-1193
  www.dunnesales.com

- **Cotton Connection**
  T – Shirts, shorts, Cotton Goods
  800-635-1104
  www.cottonconnection.com

- **Fashion Wear Plus**
  NFL, Nascar, etc. sports wear
  877-949-6060
  www.Fashionwearplus

- **Gazoz International Apparel Company**
  Jeans, Active wear, Misses, junior, men, Boys, Girls
  213-747-7777
  www.gazoz.com

- **Madison Avenue Closeouts**
  Wholesale Jeans, Dresses, Bras, Specialty Items
  704-733-9570
  www.madisonavenuecloseout.com

- **MDM International Corp.**
  Tie Dye Bonanza
  888-737-9722
  www.mdmintl.com

- **Overstock Avenue**
  Apparel, lingerie
  866-795-7990
  www.overstockavenue.com

- **Creations By Wholesale Kid**
  877-333-0117
  www.wholesalekid.com

- **Spectrum Uniforms**
  Scrubs
  713-645-3600
  www.spectrumuniforms.com

- **_Spring Import, Inc._**
  Sleep ware
  718-381-1888
  www.sprimgimportusa.com

- **_Steal Deal_**
  Men and Women's Urban Wear
  213-747-6347
  www.stealdealinc.com

- **_Thunder Sportswear_**
  Wholesale T – Shirt, blank and screen printed
  800-426-6797
  www.thundersportswear.com

- **_Wholesale Fashion_**
  Apparel, Tops, Bottoms, Dresses, Sets
  800-759-7576
  www.wholesalefashion.com

- **_Trans Am Wholesale_**
  Jeans – Men's, Women's, National & Designer Brands
  915-845-3434
  www.wholesalecentral.com/transa0001

- **_Western Express_**
  Western accessories, Hats, Western shirts, Belts, Costumes
  412-257-5020
  www.wexpress.com

- **_Wholesale Fashion Buys_**
  Women & Junior Sportswear & Fashion Apparel
  213-624-4242
  www.wholesalefashionbuys.com

- **_All Star Wholesalers_**
  Wholesale Lots, Supplies, Liquidators
  423-626-8160
  www.allstarwholesales.com

- **_Wholesales_**
  Wholesale Clothing, Auctions
  www.wholesalers.com

- **Golden Ages Group, Inc.**
  Wholesale, Fashion Tops, T-Shirts, Shorts, Pants, Jeans
  www.goldenages.us

- **Michelle & Scott's Wholesale Imports**
  Caps
  901-767-0838
  www.wholesaleImport.com/cv

- **Top Quality Sheets**
  Deluxe 6 Piece Sheet Sets, Acrylic Mink Blankets
  www.allthatjazzonline.com

- **K & C Hosiery ,LLC**
  Tall T-Shirts
  856-661-0060
  www.kchosiery.com

- **Chic Style Wholesale**
  Misses, Women, Juniors
  213-749-1026
  www.chicstylewholesale.com

- **Rose Gal**
  Korean Style Clothes
  929-800-4485 (USA)
  www.rosegal.com

- **Wholesale Central**
  Apparel
  www.wholesalecentral.com

AS SEEN ON TV

- **Wholesale Central**
  Handbags, Sporting goods, Perfume, Jewelry, Knives, Lawn & Garden
  www.wholesalecentral.com

- **EZ Wholesaler**
  Books, Movies, Music, Electronics, General Merchandise, Home furnishing, Housewares, Security.
  www.ezwholesaler.com

- *Salco Distributors, LLC*
  Over 300 As Seen On TV Products at the Wholesale Price
  800-504-2209
  www.salcodistributors.com

AUTOMOTIVE

- *Genco Marketplace*
  Auto Goods
  800-224-3141 ext.3687
  www.gencomarketplace.com

- *Main Wholesaler*
  Automotive
  800-395-1020
  www.mainwhilesaler.com

- *Fox Hill Farm, Inc. Wholesale*
  Motorcycle Items
  877-369-4455
  www.foxhillfarmwholesale.com

- *Tint-A-Shield*
  Reusable static cling UV Protector for Motorcycle, ATV, Snowmobile, Race Cars, Go-Carts
  248-931-3430
  www.tintashield.com

  Wholesale Car Covers
  Car Covers
  718-360-0700
  www.wholesalecarcovers.com

- *Wholesale Vehicle Covers*
  Car Covers
  760-752-7783
  www.wholesalevehiclecovers.com

CLOSE OUTS

- **Concord Enterprise, Inc.**
  $1.00 Items, Toys, Gift Items, Housewares, Party Goods, Closeouts
  323-588-8844
  www.dollaritem.com

- **Sav-On-Closeout**
  906-346-7065
  www.sav-on-closeouts.com

- **Brook Textiles**
  Quality Closeouts, Irregulars, Seconds
  800-251-6049
  www.brooktextiles.com

COSMETICS

- **My Wholesale Fashion**
  Cosmetics
  sales@mywholesalefashion.com
  www.mywholesalefashion.com

- **ACU**
  Lips, Eyes, Face, Nails, Accessories, Hair
  www.allcosmeticswholesale.com

- **Discounts Wholesalers, Inc.**
  Cosmetics
  610-458-1131
  www.discountwholesalersinc.com

- **Central Closeouts**
  Wholesale Cosmetics & Overstock Makeup
  888-265-6313
  www.centralcloseouts/products

- **Wholesale Cosmetics**
  Brand Name Products
  877-202-3616
  www.viatrading.com

ELF
- **_Discount Makeup_**
  _212-239-1530_
  www.eyeslipsface.com

- **_Michelle & Scott's Wholesale Imports_**
  Beauty Supplies
  _901-767-0838_
  www.wholesaleimports.com/cv

Electronics

- **_Digital Camera_**
  _604-270-3823_
  www.oxelectronics.com

- **_Price Grabber_**
  Computers, Electronics, Cameras
  www.pricegrapper.com

- **_Genco Marketplace_**
  Customer Returns, Bulk purchase only every category
  _800-224-3141_
  www.gencomarketplace.com

- **_Liquidation_**
  Electronics, Bulk Lots of Surplus, Largest online Liquidators
  www.liquidation.com

- **_Wholesale Electronics_**
  www.Wholesalecentral.com/electronics

- **_Wholesale Electronics Suppliers_**
  www.toptenwholesale.com

- **_Mega Goods_**
  Consumer Electronics
  _800-788-7518_
  www.megagoods.com

- **_Evertek_**
  Electronics Wholesale
  _951-252-8700_
  www.evertek.com/products

- **_Main Wholesales_**
  Electronics Media
  _800-395-1020_
  www.mainwholesaler.com

SHOES

- **_Marjim Shoe Co. Inc._**
  _609-407=1700_
  www.marjimshoe.com

- **_WFS_**
  Shoes
  _877-811-4911_
  www.wholesalefashionsquare.com

- **_Wholesale Fashion shoes_**
  _602-267-6477_
  www.wholesalefashionshoes.com

- **_Overstock Avenue_**
  Footwear
  _866-795-7990_
  www.overstockavenue.com

- **_Wholesalers_**
  Wholesale Shoes
  www.wholesalers.com

- **_Wholesale Shoe Warehouse_**
  #1 Wholesale Shoe Supplies
  _305-576-0077_
  www.wholesaleshoewarehouse.com

- **_Cheng's Enterprise_**
  Wholesale Easy USA Shoes
  _800-886-3288_
  www.easyusa,com

- **Sharp Men's Shoes Dress & Casual Shoes**
  Dress and Casual Shoes
  www.6PM.com

- **Wholesale Shoes-Men & Women**
  Wholesale Shoes under $10.00
  www.10dollarmall.com

- **eWinston USA**
  Men and Women's Shoes
  800-804-3988
  www.ewinstonusa.com

- **Nike Wholesale**
  Running and Training
  www.usd-buy.com

- **P & W Shoes New York**
  Stylish Footwear – Competitive Price
  718-366-6688
  www.nypwshoes.com

- **Wholesale Shoes**
  Tennis, Soccer, Sandals, Men's & Ladies Casual
  718-883-7500
  www.wholesaleshoes.com

- **Wholesale Fashion Shoes**
  602-267-6477
  www.wholesalefashionshoes.com

GENERAL MERCHANDISE

- **Springs Creative Products Group**
  Fabrics
  800-334-6466
  www.springcreativeproductsgroup.com

- **Gibson Holders**
  Display Holders
  800-444-2944
  www.gibsonholders.com

- **Frames USA**
  Frames and Frame Products
  800-577-5920
  www.frameusa.com

- **R & S Industries**
  Miracle Polishing Cloth
  314-781-5400
  www.miraclepolishingcloth.com

- **Hot Buy 4U**
  813-436-3392
  www.hotbuy4u.com

- **LNC Pet Supply**
  818-768-5855
  www.lncpetsupply.com

- **Buck Store**
  Dollar Store supplier
  786-439-0433
  www.buckstore.com

- **Knives, Lawn & Garden**
  www.WholesaleCentral.com

- **General Merchandise**
  www.ezwholesaler.com

- **Merling Wholesale**
  Blankets, Beach Towels, NFL, MLB, NCAA, Disney, Harley
  www.merlingwholesale.com

- **Continental Wholesale**
  Truckloads of Merchandise from Major Retailers
  800-869-7203
  www.continentalwholesale.net

- **Country Club Products**
  Sheet Sets
  908-352-5400
  www.countryclubproducts.com

- **Jacobs Trading Company**
  Customer Returns, Excess Overstock, Furniture
  www.jacobstrading.com

- **Jacobs Paradise Inc.**
  Incense Burners, Sticks, Pill Holders
  www.jacobsparadise.com

- **Michelle & Scott's Wholesale Imports**
  Gifts, Beauty Supplies, Purses, Batteries
  901-767-0838
  www.wholesaleimport.com/cv

- **Mars Distributing Inc.**
  Portable Insect Zapper
  800-301-2077
  www.suspendease.com/portablebugkillers

GIFTS

- **Concord Enterprise, Inc.**
  $1.00 Items, Toys, Gifts, Party Goods,
  323-588-8844
  www.dollaritem.com

- **Falcon Impex, Inc.**
  Gift Wrap, Bags, Paper
  888-398-5151
  www.falconimpexinc.com

- **24K Distributing**
  Lacquer Roses and Giftware
  866-768-2452
  www.24kdistributing.com

- **Wholesale Dollar Item Specialist**
  www.jcsales.com

- **All Fun Gifts**
  The One Stop Alternative Wholesaler
  www.allfungifts.com

HANDBAGS

- **MarJim Shoe Co., Inc.**
  Shoes, Boots, Handbags
  609-407-1700
  www.marjimshoe.com

- **Diva Design USA**
  Purses, Jewelry
  213-748-4212
  www.divadesignusa.com

- **Designer Purses**
  www.designerpurse.com

- **Handbags**
  www.wholesalecentral.com

- **WFS**
  Handbags etc.
  877-811-4911
  www.wholesalefashionsquare

- **Fashion World**
  Fashion Handbags, Evening Bags, Wallets
  213-663-1159
  www.handbagfashion.com

- **Fashion Angeles**
  Wholesale Clothing and Accessory Shop
  213-746-0035
  www.fashionangeles.com

- **G & C Fashion Handbags**
  213-746-0188
  www.gcfashionhandbags.com

- **Handbag Express**
  Wholesale Handbags
  800-616-1044
  www.handbagexpress.com

- **Wholesale Handbags**
  www.wholesalers.com

- **Michelle & Scott's Wholesale Imports**
  Purses
  www.wholesaleimport.com

- **Fashion Express**
  Handbags & Accessories, Hobos, Totes, Satchels
  www.fashionexpressus.com

- **Golden Resource Trading, Inc.**
  Purses
  212-695-8866
  www.Goldenresourceinc.com

- **A Whole Lotta Bags**
  Hippest to Sleekest Handbags
  207-319-2111
  www.awholelottabags.com

HARDWARE

- **Liquidation**
  Bulk Lots of Surplus (New & Returned)
  www.liquidation.com

- **Midwest Wholesale Hardware**
  Door Hardware
  www.midwestwholesale.com

- **Reiss wholesale Hardware**
  Hand tools, Power Tools and accessories
  www.reisshardware.com

- **Custom Service Hardware**
  Wholesale Hardware Pricing for Everyone
  800-882-0009
  www.cshardware.com

HERBS/VITAMINS

- **Main Wholesaler**
  Over The Counter Medicine, Energy Drinks
  800-395-1020
  www.mainwholesaler.com

- **Monterey Bay Spice Co.**
  Wholesale Bulk Herbs & Spices
  800-500-6148
  www.herbco.com/wholesaleherbs

- **Natural Partners**
  Wholesale Vitamins, Minerals, Herbs
  888-633-7620
  www.naturalpartners.com

- **Wholesale Supplement Store**
  Vitamins, Herbs & Natural Remedies
  484-668-1581
  www.wholesalesupplementstore.com

- **Natures Sunshine Products Wholesale**
  Nature's Vitamins
  888-625-7543
  www.healthywarehouse.com

- **Wholesale Fresh Herbs**
  Bulk Restaurant Quality Fresh Herbs
  866-588-6279
  www.marxfoods.com/bulk-freshherbs

- **Wholesale Vitamins & Herbs Directory**
  Vitamin & Herbs Wholesalers
  www.wholesalecentral.com/vitamin-herbs

HOME FURNISHINGS

- **Price Grabber**
  Indoor Living, Appliances
  www.pricegrabber.com

- **EZ Wholesaler**
  Home Furnishings
  www.ezwholesaler.com

- **Jacobs Trading Company**
  Customer Returns, Overstock Furniture, New Air Conditioners
  www.jacobstrading.com

- **Lifestyle Lighting**
  Specialty Lamps, Decorative Lighting
  877-274-7991
  www.lifestylelighting.com

- **Josh & Main**
  Home furnishing
  www.jossandmain.com

- **Koehler Home Décor**
  Wholesale Home Accents, furnishings,
  866-669-6536
  www.koehlerhomedecor.com

- **AFD Design Center**
  Art, Furnishings, Décor
  407-857-6000
  www.Artframedirect.com

- **Woodland Imports**
  Wholesale Supplies of Home Goods
  562-633-7612
  www.woodlandimport.com

SOCKS/ACCESSORIES

- **Fashion Angeles Wholesale Clothing**
  Accessory shop
  213-746-0188
  www.fashionangeles.com

- **Banion Trading Co.**
  Accessories
  800-366-2660
  www.baniontrading.com

- **Becker Glove International, Inc.**
  Gloves, Hats, Scarves, Bandanas
  314-298-9810
  www.beckerglove.com

- **Conklin Fashions**
  Hair Accessories
  800-437-1161
  www.wholesalejewelry.net

- **Dunne Sales, Inc.**
  Socks, T-shirts, Sweats
  828-396-1193
  www.dunnesales.com

- **Emby Hosiery Corp.**
  Socks, Gloves, Hats
  800-287-6916
  www.socksforall.com

- **Ss Import**
  Hats, Scarfs, Wallets
  www.ssimport.com

- **Inter Trade Corp**
  Socks – NFL, WBA, NCAA, MLB, NHL, Super Bowl Products
  888-595-3200
  www.intertradecorp.com

- **K&C Hosiery, LLC**
  Socks, Tall T-Shirts, Boxers
  856-661-0060   www.kchosiery.com

HOUSEWARES

- **MB Distributors, Inc.**
  Top of the Line Sheet & Towel Sets
  888-430-2779
  www.mbdistributors.com

- **Concord Enterprises, Inc.**
  Housewares, Closeouts
  323-588-8844
  www.dollaritem.com

- **Premier Products International**
  Housewares, Computers, Electronics
  813-436-3392
  www.hotbuy4u.com

- **EZ Wholesaler**
  Housewares
  www.ezwholesaler

- **Country Club Products**
  Sheet Sets – 6 different Sizes
  908-352-5400
  www.countryclubproducts.com

- **Liquidation**
  New and Returned
  Housewares-Bulk Lots of Surplus
  www.liquidation.com

- **Top Quality Sheets**
  Deluxe 6 Piece Sheet Sets, Blankets
  www.allthatjazzonline.com

CANDLE/INCENSE

HiGlow Candles
817-677-4004
www.higlowcandles.com

- **Jacobs Paradise, Inc.**
  Incense Sticks, Incense Burners
  www.jacobsparadise.com

- **Wholesale Candles & Candle Holders**
  718-874-9194
  www.acandleco.com

- **Wholesale Hub**
  Candles, Incense, Holders
  877-765-4050
  www.wholesalehub.com

- **Pure Essentials**
  Fragrance Oils, Soap Making Supplies, Lotion Creams, Candles, Potpourri, Gift Sets
  630-435-6307
  www.naturesbouquet.com/fragrances

- **Good Time Candle Co.**
  Candles, Holders, Incense, Potpourri, Vases
  www.goodtimecandle.com

- **Save ON Scents**
  Over 1500 wholesale Fragrance Oils
  www.saveonscents.com

- **OBI Imports**
  General Merchandise Wholesale Dealers, Candle & Oil Warmers
  800-894-2816
  www.obiimport.com

JEWELRY

- **Inch of Gold**
  800-854-3434
  www.inchofgold.com

- **Wholesale Central**
  Jewelry
  www.wholesalecentral.com

- **_Off Price Fashion_**
  Jewelry
  _866-856-8000_
  www.offpricefashion.com

- **_Wholesale Fashion Square_**
  Jewelry
  _877-811-4911_
  www.wholesalefashionsquare.com

- **_Wholesale Accessory shop_**
  _213-689-3250_
  www.wholesaleaccessoryshop.com

- **_Costume Jewelry_**
  Closeout Costume Jewelry
  _201-804-0111_
  www.bluebellwholesale.com

- **_Wholesale Jewelry_**
  _678-689-6890_
  www.rinadon.com

- **_Cool Jewels_**
  _954-456-5444_
  www.cooljewels.com

- **_Fashion Angeles Wholesale Clothing & Accessory shop_**
  _213-746-0035_
  www.fashionangeles.com

- **_Conklin Fashions_**
  Jewelry
  _607-967-3021_
  www.wholesalejewelry.net

- **_TEEDA_**
  Wholesale Sterling Silver Jewelry, Marcasite, CI
  _877-622-3522_
  www.teeda.com

- **_Selini Neckwear_**
  _866-955-8437_
  www.selininy.com

- **Wholesalers**
  Jewelry
  www.wholesalers.com

- **SS Import**
  Jewelry
  www.ssimport.com

- **Michelle & Scott's Wholesale Imports**
  Jewelry
  901-767-0838
  www.wholesaleimport.com/cv

- **Goldfathers Jewelry**
  Gold & Rhodium Layered Jewelry
  www.goldfathers.com

- **Firenze**
  18K Layers of Gold
  305-545-5880
  www.firenzegoldfilled.com

- **Plum Island Silver Co.**
  Sterling Silver Supplier
  800-543-7177
  www.plumislandsilver.com

KNIVES

- **Szco Supplies, Inc.**
  All Kinds
  800-232-6998
  www.szco.com

- **Wholesale Central**
  All Types
  www.wholesalecentral.com

- **Jacobs Paradise, Inc.**
  Knives
  www.jacobsparadise.com

- **CKB Products Wholesale**
  Wholesale Knives, Hunting, Pocket, Engraved
  888-252-2897
  www.ckbproducts.com/wholesaleknives

- **Wild Bill Wholesale**
  Wholesale MTech Knives
  888-922-5233
  www.wildbillwholesale.com

- **Blue Ridge Knives**
  Wholesales Knives & Swords
  276-783-6143
  www.blueridgeknives.com

- **CWS Cutlery Wholesale**
  Spring Assist, Throwing
  877-286-4139
  www.cutlerywholesale.com

- **Master Cutlery**
  Large Variety, Wholesale
  800-271-7229
  www.mastercutlery.com

- **Knife Import**
  Wholesale Knives, Swords, Daggers
  800-856-7172
  www.knifeimport.com

LEATHER

- **Western Express, Inc.**
  Country Western Accessories
  800-245-1380
  www.wexpress.com

- **Continental Belts Corp.**
  Belts, Buckles
  800-331-3777
  www.continentalbelts.com

- **JRP Western Products**
  Leather Whips, Phone Covers, Western Hats
  800-441-8268
  www.jrpwesternproducts.com

- **Abalone**
  Men's Handmade Wallets, Belts, Bags
  201-589-1922
  www.avalloneluxury.com/wholesale

- **Springfield Leather Co.**
  800-668-8518
  www.springfieldleather.com/wholesale

- **Sunset Leather**
  Wholesale Leather Products
  800-492-2244
  www.sunsetleather.com

- **My Leather**
  Wholesale Motorcycle leather Jackets, Boots, Helmets
  800-514-0544,
  www.myleather.com

- **Wholesale Leather Directory – 36 Matches**
  www.wholesalecentral.com/leather

NOVELTIES

- **Western Expressing**
  800-245-1380
  www.wexpress.com

- **Main Wholesaler**
  Novelties
  800-395-1020
  www.mainwholesaler.com

- **HPTrading – Trendz 4 All**
  Costumes, Shawls, Dresses
  877-893-5959
  www.hpfashions.com

- **Imprintable Warehouse**
  Heat Transfers, Turnkey Packages
  800-347-0068
  www.imprintables.com

- **Wholesale Directory**
  www.wholesalecentral.com/novelties

- **St. Louis Wholesale**
  Novelty Hats, NFL Wholesaler, Beanies, Blankets, Candles, Mugs etc.
  www.st.louiswholesale.com

PERFUME & FRAGRANCES

- **Q Perfumes**
  Perfume for Women & Men
  323-727-3867
  www.qperfumes.net

- **Wholesale Central**
  Perfume
  www.wholesalecentral.com/perfume

- **WFS**
  Perfumes
  877-811-4911
  www.wholesalefashionsquare.com

- **Veneto Wholesale**
  Perfume Wholesaler
  877-335-0005
  www.ud2006.com

- **A 2 Z Perfumes**
  Designer Fragrances – 90% Off
  718-984-0137
  www.a2zperfumes.net

- **Wholesale Perfume & Colognes**
  Designer Fragrances
  800-727-3867
  www.fragrancenet.com

- *Frangrance X*
  Wholesale Perfume & Colognes
  888-557-3738-opt 2
  www.fragrancex.com

- *Name Brand Perfume*
  Huge Selection
  212-967-2004
  www.namebrandsperfume.com

POSTERS/PRINTS

- *Galan Enterprise, Inc.*
  Custom Signs, Free Catalog
  800-735-7757
  www.galan.org

SELF-DEFENSE

- *EZ Wholesaler*
  Security
  www.ezwholesaler.com/security

- *Cheetah Stun Guns*
  800-864-0511
  www.jaguarimports.com

- *CWS Cutlery Wholesale*
  Self-Defense Products
  877-286-4129
  www.cutlerywholesaler.com

- *Safety Technology*
  Self-Defense & Hidden Camera
  904-720-2183
  www.safetytechnology.com

- *Self-Defense Supply*
  Air Rifles, Crossbows
  800-211-4186
  www.selfdefense.com

- **Central Florida Outlet**
  Stun Guns
  386-212-1614

SPORTING GOODS

- **Premier Products International**
  Electronic Sports Gear
  813-436-3392
  www.hotbuy4u.com

- **Casey's Distributing**
  Licensed Sports Collectibles
  800-482-3485

- **Wholesale Central**
  Sporting Goods
  www.wholesalecentral.com/sportinggoods

- **Price Grabber**
  Sporting Goods
  www.pricegrabber.com

- **Merling Wholesale**
  NFL, MLB, NCAA, HARLEY
  www.merlingwholesale.com

- **Inter Trade Corp.**
  Socks, Licensed NFL, NCAA, MLB, SUPERBOWL
  888-595-3200
  www.intertradecorp.com

- **St. Louis Wholesale**
  Sportswear, Blankets, Candles, Mugs, Watches
  www.st.louiswholesale.com

SUNGLASSES

- **Wholesale Fashion Square**
  Sunglasses
  877-811-4911
  www.wholesalefashionsquare.com

- **Conklin Fashions, Inc.**
  Sunglasses, Accessories
  800-437-1161
  www.wholesalejewelry.com

- **Michelle & Scott's wholesale Imports**
  Sunglasses
  901-767-0838
  www.wholesaleimport.com

- **Pacific Links**
  Sunglasses
  www.sunglassespacificlink.com

- **Kachina, LLC**
  Euro Eye wear
  800-550-1231
  www.kachinallc.com

- **Elite Image**
  Sunglasses
  800-340-7642
  www.eliteimagesunglasses.com

TOOLS

- **Wholesale Tool Depot**
  610-554-6830
  www.wholesaletooldepot.com

- **National Wholesale Tools**
  Hand Tools, Automotive, Power, Air,
  515-309-1750
  www.nationalwholesaletools.com

- **JCHs Tools**
  Contractors Tools, Electric
  626-755-5264
  www.jchstools.com

- **Steve's Wholesale Tools**
  800-733-0073
  www.steveswholesaletools.com

TOYS

- **Concord Enterprise, Inc.**
  Toys
  323-588-8844
  www.dollaritem.com

- **Premier Products International**
  Toys
  813-436-3392
  www.hotbuy4u.com

- **Wholesale Dollar Item Specialist**
  Toys & Gifts – Kids
  www.jcsales.com

- **Genco Marketplace**
  Toys – Customer returns,
  800-224-3141 – X 3687
  www.gencomarketplace.com

- **Toy Network, LLC**
  Electronics, Games, Dolls, Balls
  800-767-9998
  www.toynetworkllc.com

WATCHES

- **Michelle & Scott's Wholesale Imports**
  Watches
  901-767-0838
  www.wholesaleimport.com/cv

- **_Ashford_**
  Ladies & Men's Watches, New & Authentic
  _866-274-3673_
  www.ashford.com/watch

- **_Miniin The Box_**
  Watches at Wholesale Prices
  www.miniinthebox.com

- **_Geneva Wholesale_**
  Fashion Watches
  _213-748-8829_
  www.genevawatchesonline.com

- **_Time Factory, Inc._**
  Wholesale Watches
  _877-376-3786_
  www.timefactoryinc.com

WHOLESALERS

- _www.wholesalecentral.com_

- _www.ezdropshippers.com_

- _www.dropshipsource.com_

- _www.sunrisewholesalemerchandise.com_

- _www.liquidation.com_

- _www.dollartree.com_

- **_All Star Wholesales_**
  Wholesale Lots, Surplus, Liquidators
  _423-626-8160_
  www.allstarwholesalers.com

- **_A & W Surplus_**
  Dealer Auctions Live Online Every Wednesday
  www.proxibid.com

- **Crazy Deals Wholesale**
  Brand Name Merchandise by the Pallet or Truckload
  www.crazydealswholesale.com

- **Kole Imports**
  Buys & Sells Closeouts, Thousands of Items
  800-874-7766
  www.koleimports.com

- **Bargain Max, Inc.**
  Products from Target, Kmart, Walmart and Other Stores
  704-277-8007, 800-497-5986
  www.closeoutcentral.com

THE ASIAN CONNECTION

APPAREL

- **7e-Fashion China Co.**
  Brand Fashion Clothing, Dropship,
  Email-info@7e-fashion.cn
  www.koreanjapanclothing.com

- **Dear-Lover**
  Most under $5.00
  www.dear-lover.com/wholesale-dress

- **Asia Clothing**
  86-2-0-373835 09
  www.asiaclothing.net

- **East Clothes**
  Women & Men
  0086-20-81159020
  www.eastclothes.com

- www.tinydeal.com
  sales@tinydeal.com

- www.86wholesale.net
  Women & Men Clothes, Shoes
  86 20 29046712

- **Fashion 71**
  Korean Clothes-cheap, Wholesale
  www.fashion71.net

- **Clothes Cheap**
  Women & Juniors Wholesale
  0086-20-81425931
  www.clothescheap.com

- **CN Direct**
  Women's Clothing
  86-755-89619648
  www.cndirect.com

- **Xiangshan Baidu Industry Trade**
  Babies & Children's ware, Men's and Women's Garments
  86-574 65083800
  www.globalsource.com/baidu.co

- **Shantou Strongly Trading Co. Ltd.**
  Evening Gowns
  86-754-88487022
  www.globalsources.com/shantou-strong

- **Lanogold Garments(Yiwu) Co.**
  Shirts, Polos
  86-579-85955538
  www.globalsource.com/lanogold.co

- **ShanghaiKenda Textile Co.**
  Blouses, Tops, Dresses, Shirts, T-Shirts
  86 21 34720785
  www.globalsources.com/kenda.co

- **D H Gate**
  China Wholesale
  86-10-82257676
  www.dhgate.com

  Shaoxing Shuyou Textile Garment Co.
  Reflective Jackets
  86-575-84558013
  www.globalsources.com/sygarment.com

- **Ningbo Yinzhou Gold-Sun Garments Manufacturer**
  Men, Ladies, Kids, Babies Tops and Bottoms
  86-574-83086056 or 57
  www.weilcu.com

- *Shenyang Bosi Knitting*
  Knitwear
  86-24-82710607
  www.globalsources.com/shengyang-bosi.co

AUTOMOTIVE

- **Yong Kong Shengge Electric Appliance Factory**
  Gas Powered Scooter
  86-579-7192558

COSMETICS

- **Young Do Metal Ind. Co., Ltd.**
  Manicure, Pedicure Sets, Cosmetics Tools, Beauty Products
  82-31-3385715
  www.globalsources.co

ELECTRONICS

- **Sunsky Wholesale From China**
  Cameras, Smart Phones etc.
  86-755-61302080
  www.sunsky-online.com

SHOES

- *Wholesale Cheap Nike*
  Cheap Nike Shoes
  www.Fashion-Seller3.com

- *Wholesale Products*
  www.aliexpress.com

GENERAL MERCHANDISE

- **Tatung**
  Blood Pressure Monitors
  886-2 25925252 ext. 2401

- Norte Sirius Enterprise Co., Ltd.
  Massage Products, Bath Pillows, foot Massagers
  866-2 2221 8779
  www.sirius.com.tw

- **Ian Chyng Co., Ltd.**
  Document Folders, Twin Pocket Portfolios, Etc.
  886-6 221-9856
  www.sztop-stationery.com

- **Jin Gi Industrial Co., Ltd.**
  Pens
  886-2 2246 0168
  www.opus88.com.tw

- **Arico Pen Industrial Limited**
  Ball Pen with Digital Thermometer and Light
  852 2407-7102
  www.aricopen.com.hk

HANDBAGS

- **Kangmao Arts & Crafts Co., Ltd**
  Shopping Bags, Sports Bags, Travel Bags, Canvas
  86-396-2896510

- Handbags Design N Wholesale
  Italian Leather
  0086-20-363-40781
  www.handbagsdesignnwholesale.com

Italian Leather
0086 20 2986 7585
www.italybagshoe.com

- **Sisters Co. Ltd.**
  Fashion Bags, Totes
  886-2 2231 4823
  www.sisters.com.tw

SPORTING GOODS

- **Ningbo Tenlong Outdoor Implement Co., Ltd.**
  Flashlights, Outdoor Equipment
  86-574 88193888
  www.wolf-light.com.cn

WATCHES

- **D H Gate**
  Wholesale Watches
  86-822-57676
  www.dhgate.com/wholesale

WHOLESALERS

- **H K T D C**
  Hong Kong Supplier
  www.hktdc.com

- *www.emninternationsl.com*

- *www.hongkong.manufacturers.globalsources.com*

- *www.koreanjapanclothing.com*

- *www.getthatwholesale.com*

www.ingramcontent.com/pod-product-compliance
Lightning Source LLC
Chambersburg PA
CBHW070720180526
45167CB00004B/1548